ENGLAND the culture

Erinn Banting

A Bobbie Kalman Book

The Lands, Peoples, and Cultures Series

Crabtree Publishing Company
www.crabtreebooks.com

The Lands, Peoples, and Cultures Series
Created by Bobbie Kalman

Author
Erinn Banting
Editor
Sarah Cairns
Editorial director
Kathy Middleton
Proofreader
Crystal Sikkens
Photo research
Katherine Berti
Print coordinator and
    Prepress technician
Katherine Berti

First edition:
    Coordinating editor
    Ellen Rodger
    Project editor
    Sean Charlebois
    Production coordinator
    Rosie Gowsell
    Project development, design, editing, and photo research
    First Folio Resource Group, Inc.: Erinn Banting, Quinn Banting, Molly Bennett, Tom Dart, Greg Duhaney, Jaimie Nathan, Debbie Smith, Meighan Sutherland, Anikó Szocs
    Editing
    Carolyn Black
    Consultants
    Jane Higginbottom, Alex Lloyd, Chris Stephenson

Photographs
Alamy: Robert Convery: page 11 (bottom)
AP images: dapd: page 19 (left); PR Newswire: page 29 (top);
    Max Nash: page 29 (bottom)
Keystone Press: PA Wire/PA Photos: pages 12 (top), 13,
    24 (top)
Library of Congress: pages 15 (top), 16 (top)

Shutterstock: cover, pages 4 (bottom), 7 (top), 8 (top), 9 (bottom left and right), 12 (bottom), 20, 21 (top), 22, 23 (bottom);
    aless: page 1; Bikeworldtravel: page 5 (top); Padmayogini: pages 5 (bottom), 25; Helga Esteb: page 16 (bottom); 9548315445: page 19 (right); Featureflash: page 24 (bottom)
Thinkstock: page 10 (top right)
Wikimedia Commons: Andreas F. Borchert: page 6; Thorvaldsson: page 7 (bottom); Shirley Wynne: page 8 (bottom); Rosser1954 Roger Griffith: page 9 (top); Sandyraidy: page 10 (left); Oliver Spalt: page 10 (bottom right); R. Neil Mashman: page 11 (top); Justlettersandnumbers: page 14 (top); Amanda Slater: page 14 (bottom); Rodin777: page 15 (bottom); luminarium.org: page 17 (top); Thomas Gainsborough: page 17 (bottom); J.M.W. Turner: page 18; Guy Halton: page 21 (bottom); KF: page 23 (top); Soma Orlai Petrich: page 26 (top); Charles Baughlet: page 26 (bottom); John G. Murdoch: page 27 (top); Effie: page 27 (bottom); Klow: page 28 (top); Carl Van Vechten: page 28 (bottom left); George Charles Beresford: page 28 (bottom right)
Illustrations
Jeff Crosby: pp. 30–31
Dianne Eastman: icon
David Wysotski, Allure Illustrations: back cover

Front cover: A batsman prepares to bat during a cricket game. Cricket was first played in the 1500s in southern England. By the end of the 1700s, it became England's national sport.

Title page: English soldiers dressed in red uniforms perform the Changing of the Guard ceremony at Buckingham Palace.

Icon: Westminster Abbey, which appears at the head of each section, is the oldest church in England. Construction of the church began in the 1200s.

Back cover: Red foxes live in wooded areas across England. These animals live alone unless they are raising their young.

Library and Archives Canada Cataloguing in Publication

Banting, Erinn, 1976-
    England : the culture / Erinn Banting. -- Rev. ed.

(The lands, peoples, and cultures series)
Includes index.
Issued also in electronic formats.
ISBN 978-0-7787-9828-6 (bound).--ISBN 978-0-7787-9831-6 (pbk.)

    1. England--Civilization--Juvenile literature.
I. Title. II. Series: Lands, peoples, and cultures series

DA110.B345 2012   j942   C2012-902289-6

Library of Congress Cataloging-in-Publication Data

Banting, Erinn.
    England. The culture / Erinn Banting. -- Rev. ed.
        p. cm. -- (The lands, peoples, and cultures series)
    "A Bobbie Kalman Book."
    Includes index.
    ISBN 978-0-7787-9828-6 (reinforced library binding : alk. paper) -- ISBN 978-0-7787-9831-6 (pbk. : alk. paper) -- ISBN 978-1-4271-7890-9 (electronic pdf) -- ISBN 978-1-4271-8005-6 (electronic html)
    1. England--Civilization--Juvenile literature. 2. England--Social life and customs--Juvenile literature. I. Title.

DA110.B275 2012
942--dc23   2012013776

Crabtree Publishing Company
www.crabtreebooks.com   1-800-387-7650

Printed in the U.S.A./052012/FA20120413

Published in Canada
Crabtree Publishing
616 Welland Ave.
St. Catharines, Ontario
L2M 5V6

Published in the United States
Crabtree Publishing
PMB 59051
350 Fifth Avenue, 59th Floor
New York, New York 10118

Published in the United Kingdom
Crabtree Publishing
Maritime House
Basin Road North, Hove
BN41 1WR

Published in Australia
Crabtree Publishing
3 Charles Street
Coburg North
VIC 3058

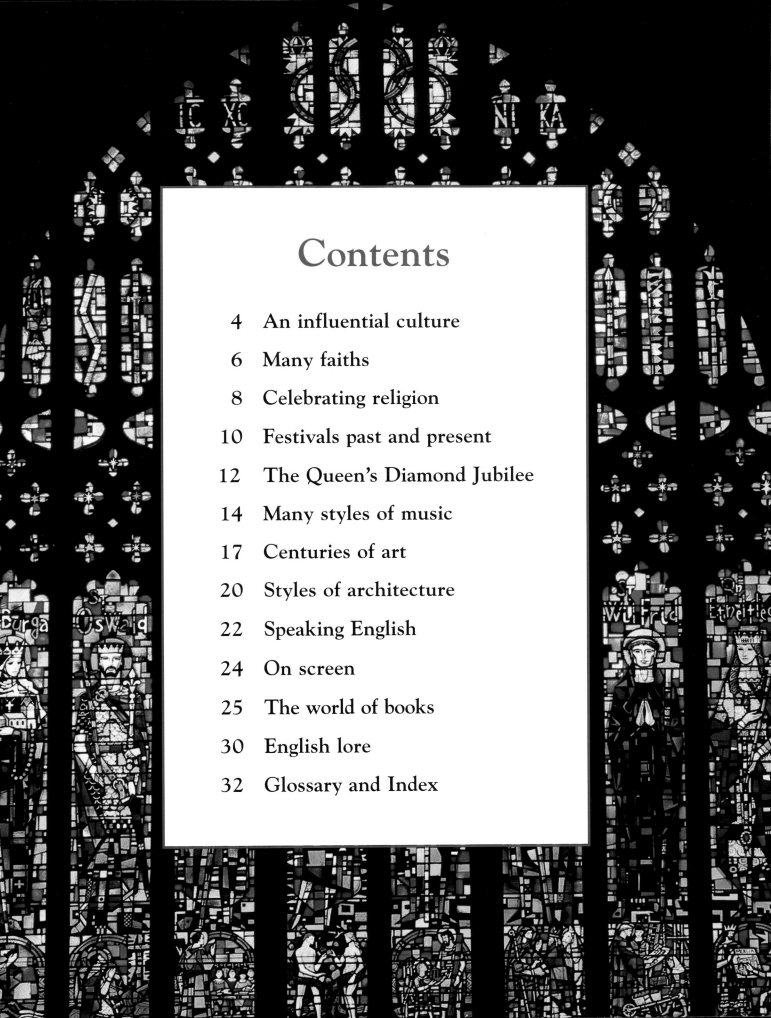

Contents

An influential culture

Throughout history, England has been one of the most influential places in the world **economically**, politically, and culturally. Sharing the island of Great Britain with Scotland and Wales, England has produced writers such as William Shakespeare, musicians such as the Beatles, and artists such as Henry Moore, who have changed literature, music, and art forever.

Outside influences

England spread its culture to the many regions it **colonized** throughout history. Among them are Scotland, Wales, and Northern Ireland, which, along with England, are part of a country called the **United Kingdom**. More recently, England's culture has been influenced by **immigrants** from other parts of Europe, Asia, Africa, North and South America, and islands in the Caribbean. All these immigrants have brought their customs and traditions with them.

Henry Moore (1898–1986) is shown here at his studio in England. Since Moore's death, his home and studio, in the eastern town of Perry Green, have been turned into a gallery.

The members of England's royal family live and work in Buckingham Palace, in London. The palace was originally built in the 1700s as a home for a noble family.

Costumed people parade down a street in London during the Notting Hill Festival, which celebrates the culture of people from the Caribbean who moved to England.

The Lord Mayor travels down Ludgate Hill in the famous golden carriage during the Lord Mayor's Parade. The parade has been held in London for nearly 800 years to honor the city's mayor.

England's early inhabitants were hunters who believed in gods and goddesses that controlled nature. They built massive stone structures where they buried their dead and performed religious ceremonies.

Celtic beliefs

The Celts, who arrived from central Europe in 700 B.C., believed there were spirits in nature, such as the water spirits Yonne and Condatis. Druids, or Celtic religious leaders, communicated with the spirits, performed **sacrifices**, and healed the sick. Some English people of Celtic **descent** still visit **sacred** pools of water, called holy wells, where they believe the water spirits lie. They leave offerings, such as coins or food, and ask the water spirits for good health or luck in love.

The Celts built holy wells, which were wells or pools of water that were sometimes sheltered by low stone structures. They left gifts at the wells for gods and goddesses, who they believed controlled nature and fortune.

Arrival of Christianity

Today, most English are Christians. Christians believe in one God and follow the teachings of his son on earth, Jesus Christ. Christianity gradually became England's official religion during the nearly 500-year rule of England by Rome, which ended in 410 A.D. Around 50 A.D., a group of people had arrived from Germany and Scandinavia, a region in northern Europe. These people, who came to be known as the Anglo-Saxons, believed in many gods and goddesses, but over time they **converted** to Christianity.

The Protestant Reformation

By the 1500s, most people in Europe practiced Roman Catholicism, the only **denomination** of Christianity at the time. Some people were unhappy with the Roman Catholic Church, and believed the Pope, the leader of the Church in Rome, had too much power. The Church controlled a lot of land all over Europe and taxed the people who lived on it heavily.

(right) Muslim women and girls cover their heads with scarves as they pray in houses of worship called mosques.

(below) People visit the shrine of Our Lady of Walsingham, in the eastern town of Little Walsingham, to ask for good health and luck with money and love. If their wishes are granted, they put up a plaque to thank Lady Walsingham for her blessings.

The Church of England

The ideas of the Reformation spread across countries in Europe where Roman Catholicism was the official religion. Henry VIII, who ruled England at the time, established the Church of England, which combined Protestant ideas and Roman Catholic traditions. Over time, several Churches developed from the Church of England. These Churches, along with the Church of England, are known as the Anglican Communion. Today, more than half of England's population belongs to the Anglican Communion.

Other religions

Different denominations of Protestantism gradually developed, including Jehovah's Witnesses and the Baptist, Methodist, Quaker, and Congregational Churches. Today, many people in England follow these religions.

Immigrants to England have brought their religions, such as Judaism, Hinduism, and Islam, with them. Jews believe in one God and follow the teachings of the Torah, their holy book. Followers of Islam are called Muslims. They believe in the teachings of God, whom they call Allah, and of his **prophets**. Hindus, mainly from India, believe in one supreme power named Brahman who is made up of three parts—Brahma, Vishnu, and Siva. These parts create, preserve, and destroy the universe.

Celebrating religion

A family exchanges gifts by the Christmas tree.

Most people in England celebrate Christian holidays, such as Christmas and Easter. Christmas, December 25, remembers the birth of Jesus Christ. Before Christmas, people send one another Christmas cards. The tradition of sending Christmas cards began in England in the 1800s, when an English businessman decided that writing Christmas letters to all his friends and relatives took too much time. He asked an artist to create a card that he could send to everyone he knew. Today, millions of Christmas cards are sent in England and around the world.

Christmas has come!
On Christmas Eve, December 24, children put letters they wrote to Father Christmas, or Santa Claus, in the fire so he can read their wishes in the smoke that rises from their chimneys. On Christmas Day, families open gifts, sing Christmas carols, and eat a large Christmas dinner. At the dinner, it is traditional for people to pull crackers, which are paper tubes decorated in colorful wrap that snap loudly when their ends are pulled. Inside are toys, paper crowns, jokes, and other gifts. Thomas Smith, who was from England, created crackers in the 1860s.

A Christmas card from the 1800s shows mistletoe, a type of plant with waxy leaves and white or red berries that people kiss under at Christmas time. The Celts used mistletoe in their religious ceremonies because they thought it was sacred. The Romans believed mistletoe was a symbol of peace.

Before Easter

Easter, which takes place in March or April, marks the death and **resurrection, or rebirth,** of Jesus Christ. On Good Friday, the day Jesus was crucified, or put to death on a cross, people eat hot cross buns after church. The tradition of eating hot cross buns started with the Anglo-Saxons, who sacrificed oxen in the spring so they would have a good harvest. Then, they ate buns marked with crosses that looked like the oxen's horns.

Easter Sunday

On Easter Sunday, children hunt for candy and chocolate eggs. They also participate in egg-rolling contests, where they try to roll brightly painted hard-boiled eggs downhill without cracking them.

Celebrating other religions

The most important holidays in the Jewish religion are *Rosh Hashanah*, which is the Jewish New Year, and *Yom Kippur*, the Day of Atonement, when people ask forgiveness for their sins. *Ramadan* is a month-long period during which Muslims fast from sunrise to sundown. The period ends with the festival of *Eid ul-Fitar*. *Diwali* is a festival of lights that marks the Hindu New Year, in October.

Children get to eat their hard-boiled eggs after the egg-rolling contest is over.

During Diwali, people light candles and oil lamps to welcome the Hindu goddess of wealth, Lakshmi.

9

Festivals past and present

Important dates in history, royal ceremonies, and changes in the seasons are all causes for celebration in England. The Jorvik Viking Festival, in the northeastern city of York, takes place each February. The Vikings were fierce warriors from Norway and Denmark. They raided England in 789 A.D. and later established settlements such as Jorvik, now called York. To celebrate the founding of their city, the citizens of York dress in traditional Viking clothing, sail reproductions of Viking boats called longboats, and reenact Viking battles.

Ancient celebrations

People gather at an ancient stone circle called Stonehenge on June 21, Midsummer Day, to celebrate the first day of summer. Thousands of years ago, druids also held ceremonies at Stonehenge to celebrate the arrival of the new season.

Celebrating the land

People in England's countryside hold festivals to celebrate the crops and **livestock, or farm animals,** important to their town or region. Nottingham, in central England, celebrates the Nottingham Goose Festival. According to a local story, the festival began when Nottingham farmers sold nearly 200,000 geese at a market one year.

Notting Hill Festival

The Notting Hill Festival, which takes place each summer in London, is a carnival that celebrates the culture of the Caribbean. It was begun by people who moved to England from Caribbean islands, such as Jamaica, Trinidad, Barbados, and the Bahamas. The festival includes lively music, parades, and dancers performing in colorful costumes. Nearby stalls sell traditional Caribbean dishes, such as jerk, a type of spicy chicken or pork that is cooked over an open fire.

Chinese New Year

Descendants of immigrants from Hong Kong and China host a large parade on the Chinese New Year, in February. London comes alive with color as giant dragons made from cloth and other materials dance through the streets and open squares. People eat traditional Chinese foods, such as dumplings and rice balls, and exchange small red envelopes filled with coins that they believe will bring luck in the new year.

People dressed as druids, or Celtic holy leaders, participate in a ceremony on Midsummer Day at Stonehenge.

Chinatown in Westminster, London, contains many Chinese restaurants and shops. The town is filled with bright lights and decorations on Chinese New year.

May Day

The Celts celebrated May 1, or May Day, with dancing, singing, and animal sacrifices to their gods and goddesses. This was meant to ensure a successful harvest in the fall. A new May Day tradition began in the **Middle Ages**, as people danced around a Maypole, which is a large pole decorated with branches, wildflowers, and flowing ribbons. People still perform dances around the Maypole on May Day.

May 1, was declared Labor Day during the 1880s, in support of workers around the world struggling for better conditions. Many countries, including England, held large Labor Day parades and protests at which people voiced their objections to poor working conditions. Today, workers march in large parades throughout England. The largest parade takes place in England's **capital**, London.

Celebrating history

November 5, Guy Fawkes Day, remembers the rebel Guy Fawkes's unsuccessful attempt at blowing up England's Parliament Building in the 1600s. Fawkes was fighting for the rights of Roman Catholics in Protestant England. Today, people celebrate the discovery of his plot by lighting bonfires, setting off fireworks, and burning stuffed "Guy" figures made of old clothes.

Children make patterns in the air with sparklers at a Guy Fawkes Day celebration.

Dancers weave long, colorful ribbons around a Maypole on Ickwell Green, in southcentral England.

The Queen's Diamond Jubilee

Many holidays honor the royal family. A royal jubilee celebrates milestones in a monarch's reign. In 2012, England's current queen, Elizabeth II, marks the 60th anniversary of her rule over the United Kingdom. She became queen on February 6, 1952, after the death of her father, King George VI. Only one other British monarch has celebrated a diamond jubilee—Queen Victoria in 1897.

Queen Elizabeth's coronation took place in Westminster Abbey, a famous cathedral in London. Crowds of people lined the streets to catch a glimpse of the new 25-year-old queen. The ceremony was broadcast worldwide via radio and, for the first time, on television.

To mark the queen's Diamond Jubilee, members of the royal family will visit every commonwealth Country in 2012. The *Central Weekend*, June 2-5, marks the official jubilee celebration and is a national public holiday in England, Scotland, and Wales. As in past jubilee celebrations, Britons will hold street parties and picnics with friends and neighbors. For the Diamond Jubilee, a parade of 1,000 boats, including a royal barge carrying the queen, will sail the River Thames. Other events will include a music concert at Buckingham Palace and a carriage procession through the streets of London.

(above) Queen Elizabeth II is shown here with her husband the Duke of Edinburgh at her coronation.

(left) Since 1066, 38 kings and queens have been crowned in Westminster Abbey in London.

In 2012, Prince Harry represented the Queen on his royal tour of Commonwealth Caribbean countries. Prince Harry, grandson of Queen Elizabeth II, is shown here taking part in Diamond Jubilee celebrations in Jamaica.

Worldwide celebrations

In honor of the Diamond Jubliee, Queen Elizabeth and her husband will tour England, Wales, and Scotland; her son Prince Charles will tour Canada, Australia, and New Zealand; her daughter Anne, the Princess Royal, will tour Mozambique and Zambia; her son Prince Andrew will visit India; and her grandson Prince William and his wife Catherine will visit Malaysia and Singapore.

Queen Elizabeth does a "walkabout" to meet children at a school in London, England, in March 2012, as part of her Diamond Jubilee tour.

Many styles of music

Minstrels, or traveling musicians, crossed the English countryside during the Middle Ages performing at markets, at fairs, and in the homes of wealthy **people**. They sang songs about love and heroes while accompanied by music played on fiddles, stringed instruments called psalteries, and fifes, which are similar to flutes.

Court musicians

Kings, queens, and other wealthy people hired musicians to compose original music for concerts and celebrations. Musician Henry Purcell (1659–1695) performed at the royal court through the reigns of three rulers. Purcell's best known composition is *Trumpet Voluntary*, named for the set of pipes, called "trumpets," on church organs. Today, musicians play this piece on both organs and trumpets.

Henry Purcell is considered to be one of the greatest English composers.

The BBC Proms is a collection of more than 70 promenade concerts held over eight weeks at the Royal Albert Hall in London. The first "Prom" was performed in 1895 to introduce people to classical music.

Gilbert and Sullivan's plays are performed throughout the world. A 1937 poster advertises a performance of The Pirates of Penzance *in Cincinnati, Ohio.*

Gilbert and Sullivan

William Schwenck Gilbert (1836–1911) and Arthur Sullivan (1842–1900) began composing music together in 1871. The duo later became famous around the world as Gilbert and Sullivan. Together, they wrote musicals, called operettas, that told humorous stories through dialogue and lively songs. Gilbert and Sullivan's most famous operetta is *The Pirates of Penzance*, about a boy who is captured and made a pirate.

Composers over the centuries

Many English composers influenced musicians around the world. Thomas Arne (1710–1778) wrote dramatic music, especially for the theater. Ralph Vaughn Williams (1872–1958) created an English style of music by writing compositions for orchestras that were influenced by English folk songs. Michael Tippett (1905–1998) wrote music inspired by religion, including African spiritual music.

Edward Elgar (1857–1934) wrote oratorios, compositions based on religious subjects, and patriotic pieces, such as marches.

The Beatles wave to fans as they arrive at the John F. Kennedy Airport in New York in 1964.

The British Invasion

English popular music changed the world in the early 1960s, when The Beatles — a band made up of John Lennon, Paul McCartney, George Harrison, and Ringo Starr — arrived in the United States to perform their smash hit song "I Want to Hold Your Hand." People everywhere loved their music, which combined folk music, rock, jazz, blues, orchestral music, and electronic sounds. The Beatles' popularity opened the door for other English bands, including The Rolling Stones, The Who, The Kinks, and Pink Floyd, who gained fans around the world. This period in music became known as "the **British** Invasion."

Pop music today

The 1970s brought a new style of music, as bands such as Led Zeppelin and Deep Purple performed loud music, called "hard rock" and "heavy metal," on guitars and drums. In the mid 1970s, punk bands, such as The Clash, shocked fans with their outrageous hairstyles, bodies pierced with safety pins, ripped clothes and army boots, and lyrics that encouraged people to challenge rules and authority. In the 1980s, less rebellious pop groups, such as the Eurythmics, Wham, UB40, and Duran Duran, became famous. Today's English bands, including Cold Play, Radiohead, Super Furry Animals, and the Chemical Brothers, create new forms of music by combining traditional, electronic, and computer-generated sounds.

English singer and songwriter Adele has become famous for her combination of soul and pop music. She's topped the charts with her hit songs both in the United Kingdom and in the United States.

Centuries of art

Some of England's earliest artists were the Beaker people, named after the beakers, or pots, they formed from clay and metal about 4,500 years ago. The Celts shaped metal into elaborate jewelry, shields, swords, helmets, and dishes. They decorated these objects with symbols, such as knots, circles, and coils. Later, the Anglo-Saxons created detailed carvings out of stone, ivory, wood, and bone. Some carvings showed scenes from the Bible or ancient **mythology**.

Honoring kings and queens

Many English artists have created works that honor England's kings and queens. Henry VIII, king from 1509 to 1547, hired German artist Hans Holbein (1497–1543) to paint pictures of the royal family. Elizabeth I, who ruled from 1558 to 1603, hired Isaac Oliver and his son Peter Oliver to paint miniatures, or small paintings, of people and religious scenes.

(below) Thomas Gainsborough (1727–1788) painted portraits and landscapes, including **Mr. and Mrs. Andrews.**

English art emerges

Everyday life in England became the subject of artwork in the 1700s. William Hogarth (1697–1764) **criticized** English society in his paintings. Joshua Reynolds (1723–1792) painted portraits of royalty and everyday people in a decorative style called rococo.

(above) English painter George Gower painted this portrait of Queen Elizabeth I to commemorate the defeat of the Spanish in 1588.

Landscape painting

John Constable (1776–1837) and Joseph Mallord Williams (J.M.W.) Turner (1775–1851) painted scenes of the English countryside. Their work is painted to look dreamy, with parts out of focus. John Constable's landscape *The Haywain*, showing a country scene with a cottage, pond, and cart, is famous for its warm, rich colors. In *Peace: Burial at Sea*, by J.M.W. Turner, it is difficult to make out the dark shape of a ship surrounded by light and blurred by fog and smoke.

J.M.W. Turner painted The Burning of the Houses of Lords and Commons, 16 October, 1834 *based on his first-hand view of the burning of the Houses of Parliament in London.*

Modern artists

Graham Sutherland (1903–1980) was an artist during World War II (1939-1945). Sutherland painted a portrait of British prime minister Winston Churchill, who was in office during the war. David Hockney (1937–) gained recognition painting in a style called pop art, which uses bright colors and sharp lines. His later works were painted in a more realistic style.

(above) David Hockney's painting A Bigger Splash *uses the bright colors of the pop art style. Hockney now lives in the United States and has painted the bright colors of swimming pools in California.*

Pottery

Many English homes have dishware, vases, and figurines made by the English companies Royal Doulton and Wedgwood. Some Royal Doulton figurines depict the mice of Brambly Edge, which are featured in a series of books by English author Jill Barklem. Wedgwood is known for a style of blue **stoneware** with raised white decorations. The pieces show scenes from mythology and from classic English novels.

Sculpture

Henry Moore (1898–1986) was an English sculptor who hoped that visitors would touch, climb, or even sit on his works. Many of his statues were titled *Reclining Figure* and depicted people sitting or lying down. Barbara Hepworth (1903–1975) created statues from wood and stone, sometimes using other materials, such as string and wire, in her work. Her sculptures, such as *Two Figures*, are known for their sleek lines.

Young British Artists

The art of "the Young British Artists" have been called everything from art to trash. Artists in the group, including Damien Hirst (1961–), Sarah Lucas (1962–), Tracey Emin (1963–), and Matt Collishaw (1966–), use paint, photography, and common objects to shock their audiences. In one exhibit, Damien Hirst displayed a **dissected** pig, and Matt Collishaw showed a photograph of a bullet in a human brain. Many countries refuse to allow the artists to display their work there.

(below) Before she died, Barbara Hepworth designed a garden filled with her sculptures, many of which were inspired by nature.

 # Styles of architecture

In the Middle Ages, kings, queens, and wealthy families built strong castles for defense. The Tower of London, which took 600 years to build, was constructed to protect the royal family and the city of London. Visitors can still see the narrow windows through which soldiers once shot arrows at attackers.

As England grew more peaceful and the need for defense lessened, many castles were turned into beautiful homes. Penshurst Palace, in southeastern England, has been home to the same family for more than 500 years. Carved pillars, which support the roof in the main hall, resemble servants who may have worked in the house hundreds of years ago.

(above) Arundel Castle was constructed in the 11th century. It was originally built as a defense for the River Arun in West Sussex and later become home to the Dukes of Norfolk.

Cathedrals

Construction on many of England's large churches, called cathedrals, began during the Middle Ages and sometimes took hundreds of years to complete. Salisbury Cathedral, in the south, was built between 1220 and 1258. Its hundreds of pointed windows and arched doorways are meant to draw people's attention upward, to the heavens.

(below) Salisbury Cathedral's flying buttresses, or arches, help hold the weight of the ceiling.

Famous architects

Inigo Jones (1573–1652) was one of England's most important **architects**. He designed churches and royal houses, such as the Queen's House, built near London between 1616 and 1635. The simple lines of this vacation home, built for Anne, the wife of King James I, were inspired by ancient Roman architecture.

Eric Parry, a London-based architect, is best known for his restoration work on one of England's famous churches St. Martin-in-the-Field and his design of one of the apartment blocks in the new Olympic Village. His style combines art and architecture to create aesthetically pleasing buildings.

Industrial buildings

During the **Industrial Revolution**, factories, **mills**, warehouses, railway stations, and docks were built to create and ship new products. Cities such as Liverpool, Leeds, Manchester, Sheffield, and Bradford showed off their new wealth by decorating new buildings with glazed tiles and elaborately carved wooden frames for doors and windows. Many of these buildings have been restored and turned into offices, theaters, lofts, and hotels.

The Lloyd's Building was completed in 1986 for the insurance company Lloyd's of London.

New developments

Architects continue to create unusual buildings in England. Designed by Richard Rogers (1933), the Lloyd's Building, in London, is sometimes called "the inside-out building" because columns, elevators, staircases, and toilets that are normally inside a building are outside, in six towers. Norman Foster (1935–) designed Stansted Airport in London to resemble its surrounding wooded fields. The airport's elaborate roof is supported by pipes branching out from steel "trees" throughout the one-story building.

The Manchester Free Trade Hall, which was built during the Industrial Revolution for public meetings, was transformed from a theater to a hotel in 2004.

Speaking English

English is the third most widely spoken language in the world. The Angles, a group that came to England in the 400s from present-day Denmark, introduced the earliest form of the language. Other languages influenced English over time, especially French. When William of Normandy became king of England, he made French the main language of his newly conquered territory. The English words "chef," "restaurant," and "marionette" were all originally French words.

Today, the Roman alphabet, which is used in the English language, has 26 letters. Before the Middle Ages, the alphabet had 23 letters. Some of these letters represented more than one sound. In the Middle Ages, "I" was separated into the letters "I" and "J," and "V" was separated into the letters "U," "V," and "W." This helped people pronounce certain words.

The *Oxford English Dictionary*

By the 1800s, most people in England spoke English, but there were different **dialects**, or versions of the language. In 1857, a group of scholars decided to make a dictionary of all English words. The **scholars** guessed that the four-volume dictionary would take four years to complete. After five years, they had only reached the word "ant." It took nearly 50 years to complete the first edition of the *Oxford English Dictionary*, which filled twelve volumes. Today, the dictionary is constantly updated and can be found in a set of 20 books, on CD-ROMs, or online.

Schoolchildren in England and other English-speaking countries use the dictionary for reference when writing essays or reports.

In England, newspapers are available in almost every language.

Regional language

People's pronunciation differs depending on where in England they live. In the east, many people drop the letter "h" from the beginnings of words, so "help" is pronounced "elp." In the southeast, people often drop the letter "r" from the ends of words, so "forever" is pronounced "forevuh." Vocabulary also differs from place to place. For example, in the western city of Liverpool, people say "gerr," which means "get."

Cockney

Cockney is a dialect of English that developed in London. No one is sure when Cockney originated, although they know it was used among traders, robbers, and pirates to communicate secretly. This dialect, which is sometimes called rhyming slang, uses rhymes. For example, if people want to say "money" in Cockney, they say "bees and honey" because "money" and "honey" rhyme. Instead of saying "tea," they say "Rosie lee" because "tea" and "lee" rhyme.

English around the world

People from North America who ask for "chips" in England receive French fries. Potato chips are called "crisps." Truck drivers in England drive "lorries," and they fill up their tanks with "petrol," or gasoline. In the following chart are other words you might hear in England.

In England	In North America
Flat	Apartment
Jumper	Sweater
Trousers	Pants
Nappies	Diapers
Lift	Elevator
Trainers	Running shoes or sneakers
Ring	Call on a telephone

A boy reads along with his grandfather. Children in England are taught to read simple words before they start school. England has one of the highest literacy rates in the world.

On screen

Famous actors

Many English actors are so well respected that the queen has awarded them the special titles of "Sir" or "Dame." Sir Laurence Olivier (1907–1989) and Sir John Gielgud (1904–2000) were best known for their work in William Shakespeare's plays. Dame Peggy Ashcroft (1907–1991) was mainly a stage actress, while Dame Judi Dench (1934–) has had a varied career on stage, in film, and on TV. In 1998, she won an **Academy Award** for best supporting actress for her portrayal of Queen Elizabeth I in the film *Shakespeare in Love.*

J.K. Rowling and Harry Potter actors, Daniel Radcliffe, Emma Watson, and Rupert Grint appear at the premiere of the last movie in the Harry Potter series.

Movies and TV shows from England are watched in hundreds of countries. One of the most popular TV shows is a soap opera about a typical English neighborhood called Coronation Street. Fans have watched the show for more than 40 years, and it is now the longest-running program in the history of television.

Making movies

English comedies, such as *Four Weddings and a Funeral* and *Shaun of the Dead*, have amused audiences around the world. England is also known for its dramatic films. *The King's Speech* and *Slumdog Millionaire* are two English dramas that have won awards for acting, directing, and even music. Movie director Alfred Hitchcock (1899-1980) thrilled audiences with his classic movies, such as *Psycho*, *Vertigo*, and *Rear Window.*

British actress Kate Winslet is an academy award winner best known for her roles in the movies Titanic, Revolutionary Road, *and* Finding Neverland.

The world of books

The tradition of storytelling stretches back thousands of years in England. The Celts told tales about gods, goddesses, and heroes, and the Anglo-Saxons played harps as they sang about brave warriors. *Beowulf*, composed in the 700s and written down in 810 A.D., is the oldest recorded British poem. The poem is about a Swedish warrior named Beowulf who saves a kingdom in Denmark from a monster named Grendel.

The Canterbury Tales

Geoffrey Chaucer (1342–1400) was a poet who wrote humorous tales about realistic characters. His book *The Canterbury Tales* describes **pilgrims** journeying to Canterbury, a city in the southeast. Along the way, this group of characters, including a **knight and a miller**, challenge each other to a storytelling contest. Their tales are told in separate sections of the book.

William Shakespeare

Some of today's most widely read plays were first performed at a small theater in London called the Globe and were written by William Shakespeare (1564–1616). He wrote more than 30 plays, including comedies, such as *Twelfth Night*, **tragedies**, such as *Romeo and Juliet*, and historical plays, such as *Richard II*. Shakespeare was also a poet whose works include a collection of 126 poems called *The Sonnets*.

Shakespeare's plays have inspired countless playwrights and filmmakers. English playwright Tom Stoppard (1937–) wrote a comedy called *Rosencrantz and Guildenstern Are Dead*, based on two characters from Shakespeare's play *Hamlet*. The musical *West Side Story* is based on *Romeo and Juliet*. It tells the story of two families at odds with each other in New York City.

The play The Tempest *is performed at Shakespeare's Globe, a reconstruction of an Elizabethan theater.*

In this painting from 1877, John Milton recites his poems to his daughters. Milton became blind in 1652, before he wrote Paradise Lost.

Charles Dickens has become one of the most well-known English authors. Many of his works have been performed on stage and hundreds have been adapted for TV and motion pictures.

Puritan literature

Puritanism was a Christian religious movement in the 1600s that encouraged people to behave in a **moral, or good,** way so they would not be punished by God. Puritan ideas influenced authors such as John Milton (1608–1674). His **epic poem** *Paradise Lost* retells the biblical story of Adam and Eve, who disobeyed God and were thrown out of Paradise. Milton's poem reminds people that going against God results in pain and hardship. John Bunyan (1628–1688) wrote *The Pilgrim's Progress*, which tells the story of a pilgrim on a journey to the Heavenly City. He encounters many obstacles along the way, but is rewarded in the end for his good behavior.

Novels

In the 1700s, Daniel Defoe (1660–1731) wrote the novel *Robinson Crusoe*. Inspired by an actual event, it tells about the life of a sailor abandoned on a deserted island. The best-known English author is Charles Dickens (1812–1870). His novels, such as *David Copperfield, A Tale of Two Cities*, and *Great Expectations*, are about life in England in the 1800s. *A Christmas Carol*, about a mean old man named Ebenezer Scrooge who hates Christmas, has become a Christmas classic.

Early women writers

Mary Shelley (1797–1851) wrote *Frankenstein* when she was only 21 years old. The novel is about a doctor who creates a monster out of dead people's body parts. Jane Austen (1775–1817) wrote popular novels, such as *Sense and Sensibility* and *Pride and Prejudice*, about the manners and customs of wealthy families. Author Marian Evans (1819–1880) used the name George Eliot when writing novels such as *Middlemarch* and *Mill on the Floss*. She found it easier to publish her work when people thought she was a man.

The Brontë sisters

Sisters Charlotte (1816–1855), Emily (1818–1848), and Anne Brontë (1820–1849) told each other stories about imaginary worlds when they were children. Later, all three became novelists. Emily Brontë's *Wuthering Heights* describes a romance between the novel's two main characters, Catherine and Heathcliff. Romance is also a theme in Charlotte's novel *Jane Eyre*, about a teacher who falls in love with her employer. Anne's novel *Agnes Grey* criticizes the lifestyle of England's upper classes as it tells the story of a governess caring for a wealthy girl.

Charles Darwin

Charles Darwin (1809–1882) changed the way people thought about how animals and humans develop with his book *Origin of Species*. Darwin argued that species evolve, or change, slowly over time and only strong species survive. He also claimed that humans likely evolved from apes. Christians were furious with Darwin's book because it went against the Bible's teachings that humans were descended from Adam and Eve.

English naturalist, Charles Darwin, published his book Origin of Species *in 1859.*

Poets

English poets, including William Wordsworth (1770–1850) and John Keats (1795–1821), were part of a movement called Romanticism. The Romantics wrote about nature and their personal experiences in a very emotional, imaginative way. Later poets, such as T.S. Eliot (1888–1965), described English society in a more realistic style. T.S. Eliot was born in the United States but later became an English citizen. His greatest poem, *The Waste Land*, described an English society that no longer had strong spiritual beliefs.

One of T.S. Eliot's collections of poems, Old Possum's Book of Practical Cats, *was turned into a musical called* Cats *by the English composer Andrew Lloyd Webber.*

(above) Sherlock Holmes is an English detective featured in the novels of Arthur Conan Doyle (1859–1930), an author from Scotland. Sherlock Holmes is so well loved in England that a museum and gift shop were built in London to honor him.

(above) When actor Orson Welles read the book War of the Worlds on the radio, some people thought that aliens were actually landing on Earth.

(right) Author Virginia Woolf, along with her husband, Leonard, established the Hogart Press to print her books and the books of other well-known English authors.

New literature

A new style of literature, called modernism, emerged in the late 1800s and early 1900s. Authors began to write in a style called "stream of consciousness." Instead of just describing actions and events, they described all the thoughts and feelings of the character who told the story. Virginia Woolf (1882–1941) used this style of **narration** in her book *To the Lighthouse*.

Science fiction

Science fiction authors in the late 1800s and early 1900s wrote imaginative novels about future worlds. Books such as *War of the Worlds* by H.G. Wells (1866–1946), *Brave New World* by Aldous Huxley (1894–1963), and *1984* by George Orwell (1903–1950) portrayed a sad and frightening future. For example, Orwell's novel *1984* described a government that controlled society by installing cameras everywhere and making people believe they were being watched all the time.

Children's books

From early fairytales to modern adventures, English authors have created some of the best-loved children's books in the world. Lewis Carroll (1832–1898) wrote *Alice in Wonderland*, the story of a girl transported into a world filled with strange characters. Children visit a magical land called Narnia in *The Lion, the Witch, and the Wardrobe*, part of the *Narnia* series by C.S. Lewis (1898–1963).

Other authors have written stories about children whose lives are filled with sadness, but who find happiness in the end. In his book *Charlie and the Chocolate Factory*, Roald Dahl (1916–1990) tells about Charlie Bucket, a very poor boy who is given a chocolate factory as a reward for his good behavior. The unhappy life of *Harry Potter*, a character in the *Harry Potter* series written by J.K. Rowling (1965–), changes when he learns how to be a wizard at the Hogwarts School of Witchcraft and Wizardry.

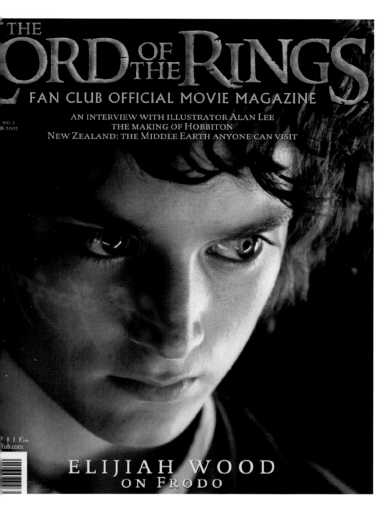

JRR Tolkien's (1892-1973) best-loved Lord of the Rings series is one of many books that have been turned into successful movies. Tolkien was born in South Africa and raised in England.

More authors

Agatha Christie (1890–1976) wrote enormously popular mysteries, including *Murder on the Orient Express*. Her novels have sold more than 100 million copies and have been translated into more than 100 languages. She also wrote *The Mousetrap*, the longest-running play in the history of English theater. It has been performed for more than 50 years nonstop, in London.

William Golding (1911–1993) wrote *Lord of the Flies*, about a group of young boys stranded on an island and forced to form their own society. This novel was made into a movie, as were other English novels such as *High Fidelity* and *About a Boy* by Nick Hornby (1957–) and *Bridget Jones's Diary* by Helen Fielding (1960–).

British author Philip Pullman's (1946-) His Dark Materials trilogy, including The Golden Compass, The Subtle Knife, *and* The Amber Spyglass, *is a popular young adults fantasy series about a coming of age story in an alternate universe.*

Some people believe that certain characters in English fairy tales and legends were real people who lived long ago. In the 1100s, Geoffrey of Monmouth wrote legends about King Arthur, who may have been a Celtic king in the 600s or 700s. One legend explains how Arthur got his magical sword, Excalibur.

The sword in the stone

The Anglo-Saxon King Uther had ruled England for many years, but he died before he could announce who would become the next king. A group of lords decided to hold a tournament, or a competition between knights, to decide the next ruler.

Sir Kay, a young knight, boasted to his younger brother, Arthur, "With my strength and quickness, I will surely win. If you help me, I will give you an important position in my court."

"What would you have me do?" Arthur asked, excited to help his brother.

"I would like you to be my squire," Kay said. Arthur was overjoyed. A squire had the important job of caring for a knight's armor and weapons. "Of course I will, Brother," Arthur agreed eagerly.

On the day of the tournament, Arthur polished Kay's armor until it shone in the sun. Then, he helped Kay put on the armor. "Where is my sword?" Kay asked.

Arthur's stomach dropped. He had forgotten the sword. Kay, furious, ordered Arthur to fetch him a sword. "I don't care if you have to run all the way home!" he hollered.

Arthur knew that he would never make it home and back in time. As he raced through the gates of the tournament grounds, he saw, to his shock and relief, a sword sticking out of a stone. In front of the stone was a sign, but Arthur had no time to read it. He pulled the sword from the stone and dashed back to Kay. "I will return the sword when Kay has won," Arthur promised himself.

When Kay's father, Sir Ecton, saw Kay holding the sword, he was shocked. "Where did you get that, my son?" he asked.

"Why, Arthur found it for me," he replied.

Sir Ecton turned the sword over in Kay's hands. On it was an inscription that read: "Whosoever draws this sword shall be the king of England." Arthur gasped. It could not be so.

Sir Ecton called the lords of the tournament together to see the sword. "How can this be?" inquired one lord. "Knights far more powerful than this small boy have tried to remove the sword and failed."

"What are you talking about?" asked Kay.

"This is Excalibur, the enchanted sword," explained Sir Ecton. "The wizard Merlin placed the sword in the stone and put a spell on it so that only the true **heir** to the throne could remove it."

Sir Ecton looked with amazement at his youngest son and said proudly, "Arthur is our new king."

Glossary

Academy Award An American film award

architect A person who designs buildings

British Relating to Great Britain

capital A city where the government of a state or country is located

colonize To establish and control a settlement in a distant country

convert To change one's religion

criticize To judge the good and bad in something

denomination An organized religious group within a faith

descent Ethnic background

dissect To cut apart

economically Relating to the way a country organizes and manages its businesses, industries, and money

epic poem A long poem that tells of heroic deeds

heir A person who receives the property or title of another when that person dies

immigrant A person who settles in another country

Industrial Revolution The shift from an agricultural society to a society that produced goods in factories

knight A soldier in the Middle Ages who fought on horseback, usually with a sword

Middle Ages The period in western European history from about 500 A.D. to 1500 A.D.

mill A building where grain is ground into flour

miller A person who operates a mill

mythology A collection of stories about a people's history, gods, goddesses, and heroes

narration The telling of a story

pilgrim A person who makes a religious journey to a sacred place

prophet A person who is believed to speak on behalf of God

sacred Having special religious significance

sacrifice To kill in a religious ceremony as an offering to the gods

scholar A very knowledgeable person

science fiction Made-up stories and movies based on space

stoneware A heavy, colored pottery

theologian A person who studies God and religion

tragedy A book, movie, or play, in which the main character is brought to ruin and suffers

Index